EUCHARISTIC APOSTLES
OF
THE DIVINE MERCY

CENACLE FORMATION MANUAL II

Eucharistic Apostles of The Divine Mercy

Cenacle Formation Manual II

Bryan and Susan Thatcher
With Seraphim Michalenko, M.I.C.

Marian Fathers of The Immaculate Conception
Stockbridge, Massachusetts 01263
2014

Copyright © 2011 Marian Fathers of the Immaculate Conception of the B.V.M.
All rights reserved.

Available from:
Marian Helpers Center
Stockbridge, MA 01263

Prayerline: 1-800-804-3823
Orderline: 1-800-462-7426
Website: www.marian.org

Imprimi Potest:
Very Rev. Walter M. Dziordz, MIC
Provincial Superior

Stockbridge, Massachusetts
January 2002

Library of Congress Catalog Number: 2002103560

ISBN: 978-0-944203-69-9

Cover Design: Bill Sosa

For texts from the English Edition of *Diary of St. Maria Faustina Kowalska*

Nihil Obstat:
Rev. Richard Drabik, MIC
Censor

Printed in the United States of America

Bibliography

Division of Christian Education of the National Council of the Churches of Christ in the U.S.A. *New revised Standard Version Bible*. Copyright © 1987.

Kowalska, Faustina M., Saint. *Diary: Divine Mercy in my Soul*. Copyright © 1987 Congregation of Marians of the Immaculate conception. Marian Press, Stockbridge, MA 01263.

Libreria Editrice Vaticana. *Catechism of the Catholic Church for the United States of America* English translation. Copyright © 1994 United States Catholic Conference, Inc. Ligouri Publications, One Ligouri Drive, Ligouri, MO 63057-9999

John Paul II, Pope, *The Mercy of God (Dives in Misericordia) Encyclical Letter*. English translation from the Vatican. Daughters of Saint Paul. Pauline Books & Media, 50 Saint Paul's avenue, Boston, Massachusetts 02130.

If any copyrighted materials have been inadvertently used in this book without proper credit being given, please notify the Copyright Office at the Association of Marian Helpers in writing so that future printings of this book may be corrected accordingly.

Mission Statement

The **Eucharistic Apostles of The Divine Mercy,** under the patronage of "the Entirely Perfect Virgin, Holy Mary" of Guadalupe, is a Roman Catholic, non-profit apostolate of the Marian Fathers of The Immaculate Conception of the B.V.M., headquartered in Stockbridge, Massachusetts, U.S.A.

Our Mission:

1) To profess and proclaim the truth of the Real Presence of Jesus in the Most Holy Eucharist, and to promote, insofar as possible, Perpetual Adoration of the Most Blessed Sacrament and the hourly offering of The Divine Mercy Chaplet for the dying;

2) To bring to a hurting world The Divine Mercy Message and Devotion according to the revelations granted to the Church through Saint Faustina Kowalska;

3) To form small faith groups, called *cenacle*s, which meet;

   a) To pray for and encourage vocations to the priesthood and the religious life;

   b) To pray and work for an end to the scourge of abortion in the world;

   c) To experience the splendor of our Catholic Faith through the study of Sacred Scripture, the *Catechism of the Catholic Church*, and the *Diary of Saint Faustina Kowalska*;

4) To encourage members in the exercise of the Faith through the spiritual and corporal works of mercy, and to help people to become sensitive to the gift and beauty of all life, especially through care for the "lepers" of today – the rejected, the lonely, the disabled, the elderly, and the dying.

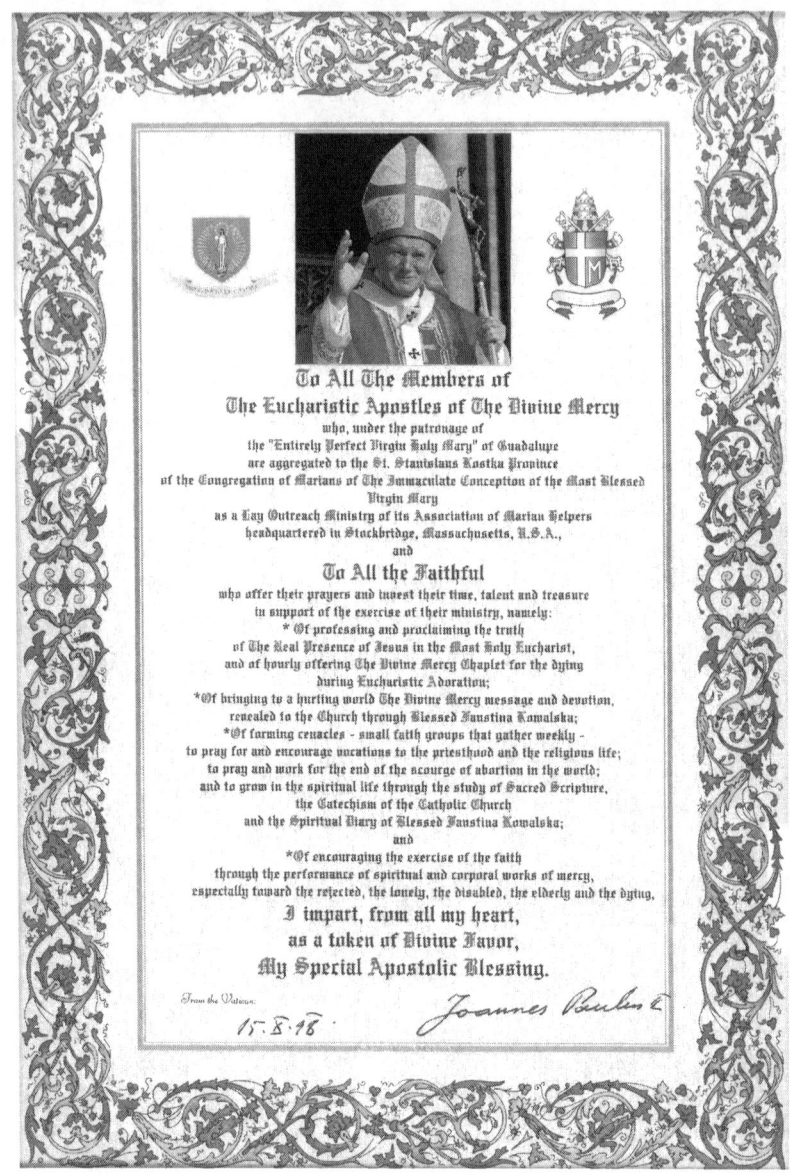

On October 15, 1998, by means of a document which he personally signed, the Holy Father, Pope John Paul II, imparted a special Apostolic Blessing to all members of the Eucharistic Apostles of The Divine Mercy, and to all the Faithful, who offer their prayers and invest their time, talent and treasure in support of the exercise of this ministry.

Dedication

This Cenacle Formation Manual and Prayer Book is dedicated to Jesus, The Divine Mercy in human flesh, whose love for us never ends, and is most present in our darkest moments; and to Mary, the Mother of the Blessed Sacrament. Through her intercession as Our Lady of Guadalupe, may all come to a deeper appreciation of the gift and sanctity of life.

May all who need healing come to the Merciful Physician.

CONTENTS

Preface 13

PART ONE: SPIRITUALITY

Humility...15

Trust and Our Call to Holiness...21

PART TWO: WEEKLY CENACLE FORMATION SCHEDULES

Week 51 23
Week 52 24
Week 53 25
Week 54 26
Week 55 27
Week 56 28
Week 57 29
Week 58 30
Week 59 31
Week 60 32
Week 61 33
Week 62 34
Week 63 35
Week 64 36
Week 65 37
Week 66 38
Week 67 39
Week 68 40
Week 69 41
Week 70 42
Week 71 43
Week 72 44
Week 73 45
Week 74 46
Week 75 47
Week 76 48
Week 77 49
Week 78 50
Week 79 51
Week 80 52
Week 81 53
Week 82 54
Week 83 55
Week 84 56

Week 85	57
Week 86	58
Week 87	59
Week 88	60
Week 89	61
Week 90	62
Week 91	63
Week 92	64
Week 93	65
Week 94	66
Week 95	67
Week 96	68
Week 97	69
Week 98	70
Week 99	71
Week 100	72

Preface

The concept of Small Christian Communities, where the faith is instilled and deepened in those gathered in an atmosphere of song, prayer, sharing, and fellowship, is nothing new. The early Church started with only twelve apostles and a few hundred disciples, yet converts were added to it daily. *"They devoted themselves to the Apostles' teaching and fellowship, to the breaking of bread and the prayers"* (Acts 2:42). It is stated eloquently in the letter to the Hebrews, *"Let us hold fast to the confession of our hope without wavering, for He who has promised is faithful; and let us consider how to provoke one another to love and good deeds, not neglecting to meet together, as is the habit of some, but encouraging one another, and all the more as you see the Day approaching"* (Heb 10:23-25).

It is appropriate that the Eucharistic Apostles of The Divine Mercy be aggregated to the Marian Fathers of The Immaculate Conception, as the mission statement of the apostolate is consonant with the charisms of the Marians.

On October 27, 1910, the renovator of our congregation, Blessed George Matulaitis, wrote in his spiritual diary:

"How much good laymen and laywomen could do if they were only instructed and enlightened beforehand in matters of faith, informed about the needs of the Church, enkindled with the fire of holy zeal and then organized into groups and attracted to the work of spreading the Faith! They would be able to bring Christ in to places we priests could not even approach."

The Directory of our congregation acts upon this desire of our Father Renovator in two numbers:

No. 84: The lay Christian faithful are to be prepared assiduously for the apostolate... First of all, they are to be helped to acquire a deeper knowledge of Sacred Scripture and Catholic Doctrine, to nourish their spiritual life and to rightly understand world conditions.

No. 85: The Congregation should take care that the people dedicated to it be joined more closely with it in an association of co-workers, that it may take advantage of their help in apostolic works and share with them its spiritual goods.

The Holy Father, Pope John Paul II, challenged us during his address to our general chapters in 1987 and 1993 with the following words:

"Modern society presents new miseries and new kinds of poverty, persons who suffer isolation, families and populations which are the victims of incessant socio-economic and cultural changes, and which are discouraged by the injustices inflicted upon them, to the point that they often lose sight of the true sense and the authentic values of life... You, Marian Fathers... let yourselves be drawn to the swelling ranks of the new poor of various cultures, so as to be able to respond to their deepest aspirations, their thirst for truth, justice, and love... "

I encourage members to be faithful to the mission statement and formation guidelines, and to be the hands and feet of Jesus to other cenacle members, as well as to the local church. Under the direction of the local priest, discern how your group can build up the church, realizing that we are all called to spread the Good News by the way we live our Christian lives. The efforts of the Eucharistic Apostles of The Divine Mercy, to enrich and deepen the spirituality and ministry of its members, affirms our motto, For Christ and the Church.

May our Merciful Savior and Our Lady, Mother of Mercy, watch over and guide your efforts.

Yours in the Merciful Heart of Jesus,

Fr. Seraphim Michalenko, MIC
National Shrine of The Divine Mercy

PART ONE: SPIRITUALITY

Humility

Humility is the virtue recognizing our dependence on God, and also the virtue most pleasing to God, and paramount to spiritual growth. On the Feast of the Immaculate Conception, Saint Faustina saw the Blessed Mother who said to her, " 'I desire, my dearly beloved daughter, that you practice the three virtues that are dearest to me — and most pleasing to God. The first is humility, humility, and once again humility; the second virtue, purity; the third virtue, love of God. As my daughter, you must especially radiate with these virtues.' When the conversation ended, she pressed me to her heart and disappeared" (*Diary*, 1415). On another occasion, Saint Faustina wrote "humility, humility, and ever humility, as we can do nothing ourselves; all is purely and simply God's grace" (*Diary,* 55).

The Blessed Mother gave a beautiful example of humility at the Incarnation when she replied, *"Behold, I am the handmaid of the Lord; let it be to me according to your word"* (Lk 1:38). While Mary wondered how all this could be as she had no husband, she recognized God's will. She did not answer with false humility saying, "I could never do that as I am not worthy," but instead, with true humility, she gave a "Yes!" for she realized that it was God's plan, and that with God all things are possible.

Saying no to God's plan for us is false pride, not humility. Even St. Faustina struggled with doubts that she could accomplish all that the Lord was asking. She wrote, "During a meditation on humility, an old doubt returned: that a soul as miserable as mine could not carry out the task which the Lord was demanding [of me]. Just as I was analyzing this doubt, the priest who was conducting the retreat interrupted his train of thought and spoke about the very thing I was having doubts about; namely, that God usually chooses the weakest and simplest souls as tools for His greatest works; that we can see that this is an undeniable truth when we look at the men He chose to be His apostles; or again, when we look at the history of the Church and see what great works were done by souls that were the least capable of accomplishing them; for it is just in this way that God's works are revealed for what they are, the works of God. When my doubt had completely disappeared, the priest resumed his conference on humility" (*Diary*, 464).

Humility can be a positive fruit of a trial and tribulation as one journeys down the winding and tortuous road of life. Such a trial or crisis might include the death of a loved one, alcoholism, financial ruin, or any one of life's disasters that we may face. Prior to the crisis, one thinks, "life is great!" At this point in time, there is little need for God. However, when troubles begin, the soul begins to question, "Is this what life is about?" It is at this vulnerable time in life that one begins to see the lunacy of materialism, consumerism, and the world's all consuming vice of pride. The soul wonders "How did I get myself into this mess?" Or "Why me, what did I do to deserve this?" As the soul tries to cope and handle the stress of the crisis, it can choose to rely on old methods that have previously failed, or it can turn to God and ask for help. If it turns to God, a stage of conversion or purgation and spiritual growth results. As the soul struggles to find itself, the saying "when the student is ready, the teacher can teach" rings ever true. The soul has a burning desire to get closer to God, and yet it is afraid, as it wonders, "Will God accept me, will He take me back?" It is these souls that God receives with open arms and a compassionate heart. Our Lord reminds us that He did *"not come to call the righteous, but sinners to repentance"* (Lk 5:32). As the soul begins the arduous tasks of healing and moving forward, it begins to grow and cleanse itself of the excess baggage that it has accumulated. With that purging evolves a desire to only do only the will of God in this life.

Even though the spirit is strong, the flesh is weak. The soul still falls into old ways and sins. Discouragement ensues as it sees little spiritual progress. It realizes that because of sin, it needs to go to the Sacrament of Reconciliation and seek peace with God. St. Faustina encouraged openness and honesty when we go to the Sacrament, writing, "a soul does not benefit as it should from the sacrament of confession if it is not humble. Pride keeps it in the darkness. The soul neither knows how, nor is it willing, to probe with precision the depths of its own misery. It puts on a mask and avoids everything that might bring it recovery" (*Diary*, 113). These last words ring of truth; the soul avoids the discomfort of probing the depths of it misery, and by doing so, it stays in the same rut and does not spiritually grow. We all put on masks, yet the God of Mercy can read our hearts. We are only fooling ourselves, not God. It is when we allow ourselves to be vulnerable that God, as the Great Physician, can heal us.

In today's world of consumerism and materialism, humility is often viewed as a sign of weakness. Being meek and humble of heart is not a weakness! Scripture tells us *"... whoever exalts himself will be humbled, and whoever humbles himself will be exalted"* (Mt 23:12). But do we really believe it, and even more importantly, do we practice it?

Pride, the vice involved and the opposite of humility, is the weakness! In spite of material wealth, it is the proud person who is spiritually bankrupt. Our Lord told St. Faustina, **The torrents of grace inundate humble souls. The proud remain always in poverty and misery, because My grace turns away from them to humble souls** (*Diary*, 1602). In our society, we are taught to be proud of many things: for example, our home, our children, and our work. It is certainly right to be thankful to God for graces bestowed. However, as time goes on, many carry things to the extreme, believing that good things are a result of superiority and talent and, of their own doing. After all, what do we have that is not a gift from God? As all good comes from Him — life itself, natural talents, opportunities, the help of others — so the only thing we can really offer back to Him are His own blessings and graces.

How many occasions, even on a daily basis, do we have the opportunity to practice humility? How many times do we have the chance to let others be first in line? In retrospect, how many times should we have held our tongue and not tried to win an argument? In today's society, winning is everything, no matter what the cost. The message conveyed is that "the one with the most toys wins." Yet, in God's eyes, it is the simple and humble soul that is most pleasing to Him. For that soul does things out of love for Him, recognizing that loving Him with our whole heart, our whole mind, and our whole body is what is most important. Father Sopocko, St. Faustina's spiritual director, told her, "Without humility, we cannot be pleasing to God. Practice the third degree of humility; that is, not only must one refrain from explaining and defending oneself when reproached with something, but one should rejoice at the humiliation" (*Diary*, 270).

How do we replace pride with humility? One way is to strive to be a servant of others, and look for small occasions daily to help others. Make an effort to see the beauty and presence of God in others. Battle against the notions that you "deserve" the closest parking place, that you "deserve" to be seated quickly at a restaurant with a waiting list, and that you can arrive at a dinner gathering whenever you get there. *"Clothe yourselves with humility toward one another, for 'God opposes the proud, but gives grace to the humble'"* (1 Pet 5:5). Another helpful exercise is a daily inventory of our relationship with God. When reflecting back on the day, did our daily actions give honor and glory to God?

The humble person also avoids being judgmental, as he knows he is a sinner and everything good comes from God. Saint Faustina wrote, "I must never judge anyone, but look at others with leniency and at myself with severity. I must refer everything to God…" (*Diary*, 253). How easy it is for us to always criticize and condemn others; how easily we overlook our own glaring faults. Ironically, God often uses the weakest to carry His message, as the repentant sinner recognizes his shortcomings and is more open to using all his time, talent, and treasure for the Lord. Scripture says *"Judge not, so that you be not judged. For with the judgment you pronounce you will be judged, and the measure you give will be the measure you get. Why do you see the speck in your neighbor's eye, but do not notice the log in your own eye?"* (Mt 7:1-3).

Paul wrote, *"For consider your call, brethren; not many of you were wise according to human standards, not many were powerful, not many were of noble birth; but God chose what is foolish in the world to shame the wise, God chose what is weak in the world to shame the strong; God chose what is low and despised in the world, even things that are not, to bring to nothing things that are, so that no human being might boast in the presence of God. He is the source of your life in Christ Jesus, whom God made our wisdom, our righteousness and sanctification and redemption; therefore, as it is written, 'Let him who boasts, boast of the Lord'"* (1 Cor 1:26-31).

The humble person is in the world but not part of it; he has detachment from worldly things and recognizes that the lasting pearl is the kingdom of God. Our Lord spoke on this to St. Faustina and said, **Today, penetrate into the spirit of My**

poverty and arrange everything in such a way that the most destitute will have no reason to envy you. I find pleasure, not in large buildings and magnificent structures, but in a pure and humble heart (*Diary*, 532). *"God opposes the proud, but gives grace to the humble"* (Jas 4:6).

We are called to do all things with a humble and contrite heart. St. John the Baptist said, *"He must increase, but I must decrease"* (Jn 3:30). As we become more aware of our failings and shortcomings, we need only pray, *"Lord I am not worthy to have you come under my roof; but only speak the word, and my servant will be healed"* (Mt 8:8).

Trust and Our Call to Holiness

Today's topic for discussion will be on trust and our own call to holiness. When one reads about the life of St. Faustina, particularly excerpts from her *Diary*, *Divine Mercy in My Soul*, one finds two elements, or characteristics, of St. Faustina that we all desire and need — a deep trust in God, as well as a sense of thanksgiving to God for His unfathomable mercy.

Did you ever reflect on the frustration that Jesus must have had as He tried to get the disciples to understand the love of the Father? And, how much sadness Jesus must have felt, as He couldn't show the Father's love to everyone? And yet, Jesus promised to send the Spirit to guide those who would say yes to His plan. Like Saint Faustina, we must say yes and strive to be saints. For, we are all called to be saints!

We are to be models of holiness, walking in union with Christ, and being faithful to the inspiration of the Holy Spirit. We read in Romans 5:5 *"and hope does not disappoint us, because God's love has been poured into our hearts through the Holy Spirit who has been given to us."* We must realize that we are members; yes, we are members of Christ making His presence known in a unique way. Remember, there is only one you, and you are a unique child of God made in His likeness and image!

We are called to imitate Christ, and allow the Holy Spirit to instill in us His gifts, and then we can become the saints God calls us to be. But DON'T WORRY! You are inadequate! For God doesn't call the qualified, he qualifies the called!

Now, we all know that St. Faustina had a deep trust in God. The major obstacle to trust is fear; the only antidote is trust. For many, the fear of something is greater than the obstacle itself. Trust — **T**otal, **R**eliance, **U**pon, **S**aving, **T**ruth (Truth, which is Jesus Christ). We must try to walk in synchrony with Our Lord, being faithful, recognizing that we do not have all the answers but trusting in Him.

In *Diary* entry #1578, Our Lord told St. Faustina, **Let souls who are striving for perfection particularly adore My mercy, because the abundance of graces which I grant them flows**

from My mercy. I desire that these souls distinguish themselves by boundless trust in My mercy. I myself will attend to the sanctification of such souls (*Diary*, 1578).

Meditate on the words of Jesus to St. Faustina, **...write that I want to pour out My divine life into human souls and sanctify them, if only they were willing to accept My grace. The greatest sinners would achieve great sanctity, if only they would trust in My mercy** (*Diary*, 1784).

Mercy is the essence of the message of God; trust is the essence of the message of us. Trust is a free act of the will, and goes well beyond feelings.

Remember the story of the ten lepers? In Luke 17:11 we read about how Jesus healed ten lepers, yet only one gave thanks to God. Jesus wants us to give thanks. Acting out of thanksgiving, St. Faustina yearns to give glory to God's mercy. In entry #1242 she wrote, " My Jesus, penetrate me through and through so that I might be able to reflect You in my whole life. ... Grant that I may have love, compassion and mercy for every soul without exception. O my Jesus, each of Your saints reflects one of Your virtues; I desire to reflect Your compassionate heart, full of mercy; I want to glorify it. Let Your mercy, O Jesus, be impressed upon my heart and soul like a seal, and this will be my badge in this life and the next. Glorifying Your mercy is the exclusive task of my life" (*Diary*, 1242).

Jesus wants us to give thanks. When we read about the miracle of the loaves, we see that Jesus took the loaves and gave thanks. The word Eucharist means "thanksgiving." In 1 Thess 5:16 we read, *"Rejoice always, pray constantly, give thanks in all circumstances, for this is the will of God in Christ Jesus for you."*

The will of God is for us to receive Jesus in the Eucharist, and then live the Eucharistic love of Jesus. We are to let Jesus migrate to every cell in our body and transform us into living icons of mercy. We are to live trust in Him in all situations. Today, let us live the message of mercy and be vessels of love to those we meet.

PART TWO: WEEKLY CENACLE FORMATION SCHEDULES

Schedule of Readings — Weeks 51-100

Week Fifty-one — *Diary,* **241-257**

ADDITIONAL READING ASSIGNMENT TO PREPARE FOR THIS WEEK:

Scripture — 1 Jn 3:17-18: 2 Cor 11:30-31
Catechism — # 2536-2538

WEEK OVERVIEW:

Envy, a sin against the Tenth Commandment, and humility, are contrasted and discussed. We are to lift up our brothers and sisters, building up the kingdom of God. We must not let envy enter our hearts, caused by our neighbor's prosperity. From it are born hatred, detraction, and displeasure. We are to rejoice in the success of others.

LEARNING AND DISCUSSION:

1) How was I helpful last week to my brothers and sisters? (*Diary*, 241)
2) Do I rejoice or become envious at other's success?
3) How is envy a sin against the Tenth Commandment?

LESSON GOALS:

At the end of the discussion, members should understand:

- How envy can insidiously enter our lives and bear bad fruit,
- The need for a deeper understanding of the virtue of humility and how to practice it,
- How we can grow spiritually and learn how to rejoice at another's success.

Week Fifty-two — *Diary*, 258-271

ADDITIONAL READING ASSIGNMENT TO PREPARE FOR THIS WEEK:

Scripture — Mt 5:3-12
Catechism — #1720-21, 1724, 2731
Article on Humility

WEEK OVERVIEW:

The theme in these readings is humility, and without it we cannot be pleasing to God. Reverend Sopocko gives Saint Faustina spiritual advice, telling her that she is to practice the third degree of humility; that is, not only is one to refrain from explaining and defending oneself when reproached with something, but one should rejoice in the humiliation. Saint Faustina also speaks of episodes of spiritual dryness. The Beatitudes and Our Lord's humility and mercy are also part of the readings.

LEARNING AND DISCUSSION:

1) Discuss the Beatitudes and Our Lord's humility and mercy; what awaits those who are persecuted for His sake?
2) Have we ever had episodes of "spiritual dryness?" (*Diary*, 268)

LESSON GOALS:

At the end of the discussion, members should understand:

- What it means to live the Beatitudes,
- The requirement to be humble, as without humility one cannot be pleasing to God,
- That if we do the work of God, we will meet opposition and undergo suffering.

Week Fifty-three — *Diary*, 272-287

ADDITIONAL READING ASSIGNMENT TO PREPARE FOR THIS WEEK:

Scripture — 1 Jn 4:7; 1 Jn 4:19-21
Catechism — # 849

WEEK OVERVIEW:

The struggles of Saint Faustina to make the interior soul a resting place for the heart of Jesus is reviewed. The role of suffering and humility in spiritual progress is again reinforced, as well as the need to love each other as we try to love the Lord. Our running from the battlefield due to mistrust is discussed.

LEARNING AND DISCUSSION:

1) How are laity part of a new community? (*Diary*, 272)
2) How do we approach our brothers and sisters in need? (*Diary*, 285)
3) In what ways do we run from the battlefield? (*Diary*, 287)

LESSON GOALS:

At the end of the discussion, members should understand:

- The role of suffering and humility in making spiritual progress,
- The need to see Jesus in others and to love them as we try to love the Lord.

Week Fifty-four — *Diary*, 288-303

ADDITIONAL READING ASSIGNMENT TO PREPARE FOR THIS WEEK:

Scripture — Acts 1:8; 1 Cor 6:19-20; Rom 8:26-27
Catechism — #684-686, 714-716

WEEK OVERVIEW:

The need to be as a little child and live life in simplicity, the human response to trials, and the need to come to Our Lord as a beggar, asking Him for graces are topics of discussions. Our Lord's explanation of the Image of Divine Mercy, as well as the promises associated with the Feast of Divine Mercy, are detailed in the readings.

LEARNING AND DISCUSSION:

1) What is our response to trials? Is it anger, acceptance, or fear? (*Diary*, 289)
2) What results if we are faithful to the inspiration of the Holy Spirit? (*Diary*, 291)
3) How are we to be like beggars? (*Diary*, 294)

LESSON GOALS:

At the end of the discussion, members should understand:

- How we can live with more simplicity and trust on a day-to-day basis,
- The promises associated with the Feast of Divine Mercy and the Image,
- A deeper realization that the Lord wants us to come to Him, asking for grace to handle our daily trials.

Week Fifty-five — *Diary*, 304-320

ADDITIONAL READING ASSIGNMENT TO PREPARE FOR THIS WEEK:

Scripture — Mt 1:20, 25:31
Catechism — #328-333, 2086

WEEK OVERVIEW:

The Passion of Our Lord, the virtue of hope, and the First Commandment are discussed. Saint Faustina's entries on the choir of angels, and the Church's teaching on angels are reviewed.

LEARNING AND DISCUSSION:

1) Saint Faustina wrote that Jesus is her only hope. How is hope embraced by the First Commandment? (*Diary*, 304)
2) She also speaks of the choir of angels. What is Church teaching on angels?
3) What did Our Lady tell her about suffering? (*Diary*, 316)

LESSON GOALS:

At the end of the discussion, members should understand:

- The necessity of hope, and living and spreading the message of Divine Mercy, and its relationship to the First Commandment,
- The existence of angels, and their role as messengers of God.

Week Fifty-six — *Diary*, 321-333

ADDITIONAL READING ASSIGNMENT TO PREPARE FOR THIS WEEK:

Scripture — 1 Jn 3:8; Jn 8:44
Catechism — #966, 974, 395-399

WEEK OVERVIEW:

This week's readings discuss the existence of hell and demons, as well as Our Blessed Mother and the Feast of the Assumption. The Image of Divine Mercy is the vessel by which people are to keep coming for graces to the fountain of mercy.

LEARNING AND DISCUSSION:

1) In entry 320, Saint Faustina is surrounded by demons. What is Church teaching on the existence of Satan and hell?
2) What is the Feast of the Assumption? (*Diary*, 1934)
3) What is the vessel by which people are to come for grace? (*Diary*, 327)

LESSON GOALS:

At the end of the discussion, members should understand:
- The vessel by which people are to keep coming to the fountain of mercy,
- The Church's teaching on the existence of hell and demons,
- The beauty of suffering united to Our Lord's suffering on the Cross.

Week Fifty-seven — *Diary*, 334-346

ADDITIONAL READING ASSIGNMENT TO PREPARE FOR THIS WEEK:

Scripture — Deut 6:4; Mt 4:10
Catechism — #1378-1381

WEEK OVERVIEW:

Topics for the week include — the Lord's request that a Feast of Mercy be established, the visions Saint Faustina had during Eucharistic Adoration, the rays of mercy emanating from the Host to the people, and how we are to let the rays of mercy pass to us and through us to others.

LEARNING AND DISCUSSION:

1) Why does the Lord want a Feast of Mercy? (*Diary*, 341)
2) What emanated from the monstrance, and why is Eucharistic Adoration important? (*Diary*, 344)

LESSON GOALS:

At the end of the discussion, members should understand:

- How we can better let the rays of mercy pass through us and radiate out to others, being vessels of mercy for Our Lord,
- A deeper appreciation of the Real Presence,
- The importance of the Feast of Mercy.

Week Fifty-eight — *Diary*, 347-358

ADDITIONAL READING ASSIGNMENT TO PREPARE FOR THIS WEEK:

Scripture — 2 Cor 4:7-16
Catechism — #202, 252-254

WEEK OVERVIEW:

The Holy Trinity, the need for zeal in our spiritual journey, and how we trust in Him on a day-to-day basis are brought up this week's readings. Saint Faustina's writings to the Blessed Host are spiritually enriching.

LEARNING AND DISCUSSION:

1) What kind of zeal should burn in our hearts? (*Diary*, 350)
2) Saint Faustina prayed in the name of the Holy Trinity; what is the Holy Trinity? (*Diary*, 355)
3) Discuss how we could have been more trusting of God since the last meeting.

LESSON GOALS:

At the end of the discussion, members should understand:

- The Church's teachings on the Trinity,
- The need for zeal in our spiritual journey as we fight for the salvation of souls, proclaiming His great mercy to the world.

Week Fifty-nine — *Diary*, 357-367

ADDITIONAL READING ASSIGNMENT TO PREPARE FOR THIS WEEK:

Scripture — 1 Cor 12:4-11
Catechism — #798-801, 183

WEEK OVERVIEW:

The gifts of the Holy Spirit, and our disposition and attitudes of caution, reservation, and mistrust to Our Lord are topics for the week. The Lord's comments to Saint Faustina on self-will and His will should be brought out in the discussion.

LEARNING AND DISCUSSION:

1) What are the gifts of the Holy Spirit?
2) How do we express caution, reservation, and mistrust to Our Lord? (*Diary*, 367)

LESSON GOALS:

At the end of the discussion, members should understand:

- The gifts of the Holy Spirit and charisms,
- How each of us exhibit mistrust and caution to Our Lord on a daily basis.

Week Sixty — *Diary*, 368-377

ADDITIONAL READING ASSIGNMENT TO PREPARE FOR THIS WEEK:

Scripture — Mk 14:3-9; Jn 2:1, 11-18
Catechism — #143, 155

WEEK OVERVIEW:

The importance of daily meditation on the Passion, the need for deeper faith, love, and trust in God, and the interior examination of conscience are part of the week's readings. The Catechism references address the great faith of Abraham.

LEARNING AND DISCUSSION:

1) How do we discern God's will? (*Diary*, 372)
2) What happens to a hard heart under the rays of mercy? (*Diary*, 370)
3) Discuss Mary Magdalene's conversion and our interior struggles to convert.

LESSON GOALS:

At the end of the discussion, members should understand:

- What happens to a hardened heart when placed under the rays of His mercy,
- How our conversion requires perseverance and trust in His mercy.

Week Sixty-one — *Diary*, 378-392

ADDITIONAL READING ASSIGNMENT TO PREPARE FOR THIS WEEK:

Scripture — Jn 8:51; Acts 5:29; Prov 21:28; Mt 6:14-15
Catechism — #16

WEEK OVERVIEW:

The promises the Lord gave to those who proclaim his mercy give all of us hope. Forgiveness and obedience are necessary in understanding the mercy of God.

LEARNING AND DISCUSSION:

1) What are the promises to those proclaiming His mercy? (*Diary*, 378)
2) Obedience to Church teaching is difficult; what does the Lord say about obedience? (*Diary*, 381)
3) Why is forgiveness important? (*Diary*, 390)

LESSON GOALS:

At the end of the discussion, members should understand:

- The promises to those who are obedient,
- The importance of our forgiving others, as this will open our hearts to God's mercy,
- An appreciation of the joy we will have as we proclaim His mercy, knowing the promises the Lord made about those who spread His mercy.

Week Sixty-two — *Diary*, 393-404

ADDITIONAL READING ASSIGNMENT TO PREPARE FOR THIS WEEK:

Scripture — Lk 16:19-31
Catechism — #543-544, 2613, 2742

WEEK OVERVIEW:

Saint Faustina writes of her visit to see her dying mother, and the lack of joy found in so many hearts. She also speaks of her father's fervor while praying, and her many opportunities presented on her trip to practice virtue.

LEARNING AND DISCUSSION:

1) Diary entry #396 speaks of a conversation with an unhappy novice who was in discernment about entering a convent. In what ways can laity encourage those discerning a religious vocation?
2) Saint Faustina writes of the fervor and sincerity of her father in prayer; is our prayer mere recitation or from the heart? (*Diary*, 398)
3) Why were the hearts of the people miserable? (*Diary*, 401)

LESSON GOALS:

At the end of the discussion, members should understand:

- That the spreading of the message of Divine Mercy should be done with joy,
- The many opportunities we each have daily to practice virtue,
- Prayer must come from the heart, and not be mere recitation of words.

Week Sixty-three — *Diary*, 405-419

ADDITIONAL READING ASSIGNMENT TO PREPARE FOR THIS WEEK:

Scripture — Lk 4:13; Mk 3:27
Catechism — #391, 393, 395

WEEK OVERVIEW:

The readings from the Diary occur during Lent, and Saint Faustina describes visions she had of our scourged Lord. The Church's teaching on the fall of the angels is part of the lesson. In the readings, she talks about Satan attacking her because of the many souls she had snatched from his dominion.

LEARNING AND DISCUSSION:

1) Jesus told Saint Faustina that Satan hates her because she snatched souls from his dominion. How can we snatch souls for Our Lord?
2) Jesus requested His image be publicly venerated. (*Diary*, 414) How can we honor this request?
3) How can we be witnesses of Jesus on a day to day basis?

LESSON GOALS:

At the end of the discussion, members should understand:

- The Church's teaching on the existence of Satan and hell,
- The need to have the Image of Divine Mercy publicly venerated,
- The need to pray more earnestly and to do works of mercy for the continued conversion of souls.

Week Sixty-four — *Diary*, 420-430

ADDITIONAL READING ASSIGNMENT TO PREPARE FOR THIS WEEK:

Scripture — Deut 6:5; Mt 22:35-40; Jn 16:26-27, Gal 5:22-3
Catechism — #736, 1832

WEEK OVERVIEW:

The writings begin on the Feast of Divine Mercy in 1935, and the Lord speaks for a need of trust in His mercy. The fruits of the Holy Spirit as apparent in Father Sopocko are also reviewed. Worldly greatness, contrasted with the Lord's requirement of humility, are part of the week's readings.

LEARNING AND DISCUSSION:

1) Why is trust in His mercy so important?
2) Father Sopocko's patience is admired (*Diary*, 422). Is patience a gift of the Holy Spirit?
3) "True greatness is in loving God and in humility," the Lord said (*Diary*, 424). In what misguided, worldly ways do we think we achieve greatness?

LESSON GOALS:

At the end of the discussion, members should understand:

- The fruits of the Holy Spirit, and where in our own lives we fall short in bearing these fruits,
- The need for humility in our lives, and although we are in the world, we are not of the world. Worldly greatness contrasts sharply with the kingdom of God.

Week Sixty-five — *Diary*, 431-444

ADDITIONAL READING ASSIGNMENT TO PREPARE FOR THIS WEEK:

Scripture — Mt 5:14-16; Mt 6:19-21; Lk 18:9-14
Catechism — #848-850

WEEK OVERVIEW:

Readings focus on how fear can cripple us from doing God's work. In spite of our weakness, the Lord will use us. We evangelize through the spiritual and corporal works of mercy.

LEARNING AND DISCUSSION:

1) The Lord told Saint Faustina to fear nothing; how can fear cripple us and prevent us from doing God's will? (*Diary*, 431)
2) Will the Lord use us in spite of our weakness? (*Diary*, 435)
3) When we do corporal works of mercy, are we allowing the rays of mercy to go out all through the world? (*Diary*, 441)

LESSON GOALS:

At the end of the discussion, members should understand:

- The need for trust, and that fear cripples us and prevents us from doing God's will,
- We are to be the hands and feet of Jesus, doing the spiritual and corporal works of mercy,
- That the Lord will use us all, in spite of our weaknesses.

Week Sixty-six — *Diary*, 445-455

ADDITIONAL READING ASSIGNMENT TO PREPARE FOR THIS WEEK:

Scripture — Lev 19:1,2; Mt 5:48
Catechism — # 946-959

WEEK OVERVIEW:

The readings address the reward given to those who suffer with Our Lord, the Communion of Saints, and Our Lady's comments to Saint Faustina on the Feast of Our Lady of Mercy.

LEARNING AND DISCUSSION:

1) Discuss the words (*Diary*, 445), "Look and see the human race in its present condition." How is the world in need of God's mercy, both on a local and international level?
2) Why is it important to pray for our clergy? (*Diary*, 446)
3) Saints are examples of holiness; what is the Communion of Saints? (Catechism #946)

LESSON GOALS:

At the end of the discussion, members should understand:

- Glory and reward awaiting those who suffer for Our Lord, who fix their gaze on His Passion,
- The Communion of Saints is the Church glorified, and we are all called to be saints.

Week Sixty-seven — *Diary*, 456-472

ADDITIONAL READING ASSIGNMENT TO PREPARE FOR THIS WEEK:

Scripture — Jer 32:40-41
Catechism — #736, 1832

WEEK OVERVIEW:

The goodness of Our Lord and His usually choosing the weakest souls are main themes. By the power of the Holy Spirit, we are able to bear good fruit.

LEARNING AND DISCUSSION:

1) How do you see the "Goodness of God" reflected in your life?
2) In what ways is God so good to you?
3) What makes us able to bear much fruit?

LESSON GOALS:

At the end of the discussion, members should understand:

- The Holy Spirit will give us power to bear good fruit and be fearless in the midst of adversity,
- If we allow, Our Lord will use all of us to promote the kingdom of God.

Week Sixty-eight — *Diary*, 473-484

ADDITIONAL READING ASSIGNMENT TO PREPARE FOR THIS WEEK:

Scripture — Wis 11:24
Catechism — #1460, 1441-1442

WEEK OVERVIEW:

This week's readings include: Saint Faustina's vision of the Angel of Divine Wrath and The Divine Mercy Chaplet; Catechism references on the Sacrament of Reconciliation, forgiveness, and silence; are other topics of discussion.

LEARNING AND DISCUSSION:

1) What prevents us from receiving God's mercy?
2) What steps can we take to become reconciled with God and the Church, and stay the wrath of God?
3) How can silence help?

LESSON GOALS:

At the end of the discussion, members should understand:

- Church teaching on the Sacrament of Reconciliation and the need for forgiveness in our lives,
- The importance of silence and listening to God.

Week Sixty-nine — *Diary*, 485-499

ADDITIONAL READING ASSIGNMENT TO PREPARE FOR THIS WEEK:

Scripture — Phil 4:10-14; Lk 22:42
Catechism — #615, 144, 301

WEEK OVERVIEW:

Saint Faustina's entries on joy, suffering, praise, and humiliation, as well as the need for obedience, are themes for the week.

LEARNING AND DISCUSSION:

1) How can we learn to accept joy or suffering with the same disposition? (*Diary*, 485)
2) Is being obedient to the voice of the Church a priority in our lives? (*Diary*, 497)
3) How can we find strength to seek God's will on a daily basis?

LESSON GOALS:

At the end of the discussion, members should understand:

- The need to accept all with the same disposition and keep our gaze fixed on the Lord,
- The need to be obedient to Church teaching and live a Sacramental life.

Week Seventy — *Diary*, 500-519

ADDITIONAL READING ASSIGNMENT TO PREPARE FOR THIS WEEK:

Scripture — 1 Sam 15:22; 2 Cor 6:4-10
Catechism — #1808, 1584

WEEK OVERVIEW:

Happiness in doing God's will and the virtue of fortitude are discussed. Also, the need to persevere amid life's struggles is referenced in Scripture.

LEARNING AND DISCUSSION:

1) Are we obedient to those in higher authority? (spiritual mentor) (*Diary*, 506)
2) Do we persevere with patience amid life's trials? (2 Cor reading)
3) How are we fulfilling God's will in our lives? (*Diary*, 515)

LESSON GOALS:

At the end of the discussion, members should understand:

- The need of fortitude to continue to try to run the good race,
- Happiness comes from doing God's will, and not from material goods, power, or prestige.

Week Seventy-one — *Diary*, 520-529

ADDITIONAL READING ASSIGNMENT TO PREPARE FOR THIS WEEK:

Scripture — Ps 103; Rom 16:25-27; Gal 2:19,20
Catechism — #2014-15, 2730

WEEK OVERVIEW:

The path of Christian holiness, spiritual dryness, and the Way of the Cross, are topics of discussion. All of us are called to the fullness of life and perfection of charity.

LEARNING AND DISCUSSION:

1) How did Saint Faustina deal with "spiritual dryness?" What does spiritual dryness mean to you?
2) Where do we get our strength to bear our crosses?
3) In what ways can we express charity to build up the Church?

LESSON GOALS:

At the end of the discussion, members should understand:

- Carrying the cross are part of our personal struggles to holiness,
- The need for perseverance as we face difficulties in prayer.

Week Seventy-two — *Diary*, 530-542

ADDITIONAL READING ASSIGNMENT TO PREPARE FOR THIS WEEK:

Scripture — Mt 6:25-34; Ps 24:3-4; Eph 5:21
Catechism — #2544-47, 2520, 2658

WEEK OVERVIEW:

The priests and religious, and the virtues of poverty and chastity are themes for the week.

LEARNING AND DISCUSSION:

1) What are the two pearls precious to Jesus' heart?
2) Discuss Saint Faustina's insights into the virtues of poverty, chastity, and obedience.
3) Can those with few material things lack spiritual poverty?

LESSON GOALS:

At the end of the discussion, members should understand:

- The need to pray for and support our priests and religious,
- The need to strive for spiritual poverty in our lives.

Week Seventy-three — *Diary*, 543-557

ADDITIONAL READING ASSIGNMENT TO PREPARE FOR THIS WEEK:

Scripture — Lk 1:45, 48; Jn 19:27
Catechism — #2517-2520, 971, 2676-78

WEEK OVERVIEW:

The readings include Church teaching on the Blessed Mother, the Rosary, and the need for trust in God in our lives.

LEARNING AND DISCUSSION:

1) The Rosary is mentioned in the readings (*Diary*, 547); why do we have a devotion to Our Lady?
2) What does the Lord promise Saint Faustina if her trust is great? (*Diary*, 548)
3) What does Saint Faustina say is needed for an offering to be pure? (*Diary*, 551)

LESSON GOALS:

At the end of the discussion, members should understand:

- Why we honor Our Blessed Mother,
- The beauty of the Rosary,
- The importance of purity of intention in our actions.

Week Seventy-four — *Diary*, 558-568

ADDITIONAL READING ASSIGNMENT TO PREPARE FOR THIS WEEK:

Scripture — Ex 20:12; James 4:11,12; Eph 6:1-3
Catechism — #491-92, 2197-2200

WEEK OVERVIEW:

The readings discuss the Immaculate Conception, judgmentalism, obedience, and the Fourth Commandment.

LEARNING AND DISCUSSION:

1) Saint Faustina speaks of being judgmental (*Diary*, 558); give examples of how laity are judgmental.
2) What is the feast of the Immaculate Conception? (*Diary*, 564)
3) What is the Fourth Commandment? (*Diary*, 567)

LESSON GOALS:

At the end of the discussion, members should understand:

- The nature of the family and the Fourth Commandment,
- The dogma of The Immaculate Conception.

Week Seventy-five — *Diary*, 569-582

ADDITIONAL READING ASSIGNMENT TO PREPARE FOR THIS WEEK:

Scripture — Phil 4:13; 1 Cor 15:10; Phil 4:13
Catechism — #1996-2003

WEEK OVERVIEW:

The Image and Feast of Divine Mercy, grace, and the pure soul, are topics included in the readings.

LEARNING AND DISCUSSION:

1) Jesus will be granting to souls more graces by means of the Image. (*Diary*, 570) What is grace?
2) The Lord told Saint Faustina that a pure soul is humble. (*Diary*, 576) How do our actions get tainted by our will and agenda?
3) Our Lord said, "If My death has not convinced you of My love, what will?" (*Diary*, 580) Do we really believe in God's love and mercy for us?

LESSON GOALS:

At the end of the discussion, members should understand:

- Many graces will be granted through the Image,
- Grace is favor, the free and undeserved help of God.

Week Seventy-six — *Diary*, 583-596

ADDITIONAL READING ASSIGNMENT TO PREPARE FOR THIS WEEK:

Scripture — 1 Pet 5:1-5
Catechism — #2540, 2094, 946-948

WEEK OVERVIEW:

The Lord tells Saint Faustina that reflection from the heart is more profitable than reading many books. Other topics discussed include humility, and envy.

LEARNING AND DISCUSSION:

1) Why is prayer and meditation from the heart necessary? (*Diary*, 584).
2) When in discernment, how is inner peace an important factor? (*Diary*, 589).
3) Contrast a proud and humble soul, and how are behavior has been since the last meeting (*Diary*, 593).

LESSON GOALS:

At the end of the discussion, members should understand:

- The importance of prayer and meditation from the heart,
- The sin of envy.

Week Seventy-seven — *Diary*, 597-609

ADDITIONAL READING ASSIGNMENT TO PREPARE FOR THIS WEEK:

Scripture — Rom 6:2
Catechism — #2742

WEEK OVERVIEW:

The writings for the week address the interior struggles of the soul. She implores all souls to trust in His mercy, especially at the hour of death. The need for patience in adversity is emphasized.

LEARNING AND DISCUSSION:

1) How did Saint Faustina aid someone who asked her for prayer? (*Diary*, 596, 604)
2) Discuss her words, "Patience in adversity gives power to the soul" (*Diary*, 607).
3) Saint Faustina writes that the Father will glorify our soul to the extent that He sees in us a resemblance to His Son. What does that say about the role of suffering and the importance of charity?

LESSON GOALS:

At the end of the discussion, members should understand:

- The need for patience in times of difficulty, as we wait on the Lord,
- How we are to be the reflection of Jesus in our daily life.

Week Seventy-eight — *Diary*, 610-624

ADDITIONAL READING ASSIGNMENT TO PREPARE FOR THIS WEEK:

Scripture — Mk 3:35; Jn 4:34,
Catechism — #2825, 1030-1032, 893, 1324-1327

WEEK OVERVIEW:

The reading discusses the power of the Eucharist, the power of prayer for the souls in purgatory, and obedience to His will.

LEARNING AND DISCUSSION:

1) What did Saint Faustina resolve to do when she understood what the Lord was asking of her? (*Diary*, 615, 787)
2) Discuss how you can seek His will. (prayer, study, direction of advisor) Why is obedience at times difficult?
3) Why do we pray for the souls in purgatory?

LESSON GOALS:

At the end of the discussion, members should understand:

- The great gift of the Eucharist,
- Why we pray for the souls in purgatory,
- The importance of trying to do His will.

Week Seventy-nine — *Diary*, 625-639

ADDITIONAL READING ASSIGNMENT TO PREPARE FOR THIS WEEK:

Scripture — Heb 10:5-9, 10:30-31, 11:6; Ps 27
Catechism — #161, 164, 2447, 334-346

WEEK OVERVIEW:

Our Lady's comments to Saint Faustina, how disbelief wounds Our Lord, and angels are topics of the week's readings.

LEARNING AND DISCUSSION:

1) How does disbelief, or lack of faith in His mercy, hinder our spiritual growth? (*Diary*, 628).
2) How can we prepare ourselves, and others, for His second coming? (*Diary*, 635).
3) Discuss how the mercy of the Lord is the greatest of all His works. (*Diary*, 637).

LESSON GOALS:

At the end of the discussion, members should understand:

- Trust must overshadow our lack of comprehension and disbelief,
- We are all called to proclaim His mercy and prepare for the second coming of God,
- The existence of angels.

Week Eighty— *Diary*, 640-648

ADDITIONAL READING ASSIGNMENT TO PREPARE FOR THIS WEEK:

Scripture — Phil 2:1-11; Eph 6:5-9; Lk 2:51; Gal 5:24
Catechism — #2544-45

WEEK OVERVIEW:

Topics for the week include sacrifice, attachment to worldly things, and conversations with Our Lord about her spiritual director are discussed.

LEARNING AND DISCUSSION:

1) What are the attachments that need to be emptied in our lives in order for us to be more useful to others? (*Diary*, 641)
2) Describe some of the inner struggles Saint Faustina was going through in paragraphs 645-647. What did our Lord tell her to tell the confessor? (*Diary*, 645)
3) What are our goals in life? Are they for material or spiritual things?

LESSON GOALS:

At the end of the discussion, members should understand:

- About poverty of heart, and what we must do to become useful to the Church,
- Why the Lord desires mercy and not sacrifice,
- How attainment of worldly goods can make it more difficult to focus on the spiritual realm.

Week Eighty-one — *Diary*, 649-665

ADDITIONAL READING ASSIGNMENT TO PREPARE FOR THIS WEEK:

Scripture — Jn 15:8; Lk 11:13; Mt 7:21
Catechism — #737, 741-47

WEEK OVERVIEW:

The lesson reviews the need for mercy in our lives and the power of the Holy Spirit.

LEARNING AND DISCUSSION:

1) Saint Faustina wrote, "mercy is the flower of love" (*Diary*, 651). How can the group show mercy locally to build up the Body of Christ?
2) Father Andraz wrote that Sister's principal spiritual director was the Holy Spirit (*Diary*, 658). What is the mission of the Holy Spirit?
3) Discuss Sister's writing, "It is the works that have come from us that will speak about us" (*Diary*, 663).

LESSON GOALS:

At the end of the discussion, members should understand:

- That mercy to those around us is the fullest expression of God's love,
- The mission of the Holy Spirit,
- The importance of reaching out through works of mercy.

Week Eighty-two — *Diary*, 666-683

ADDITIONAL READING ASSIGNMENT TO PREPARE FOR THIS WEEK:

Scripture — Ex 20:2-5; Lk 10:18; Jas 5:19
Catechism — #2083-84, 2089

WEEK OVERVIEW:

The striving to do God's will, the role of suffering, Saint Faustina's desire to save souls, and the First Commandment, are reviewed this week.

LEARNING AND DISCUSSION:

1) Sister wrote that all striving for perfection and sanctity consists in doing God's will. Lucifer had great light, but did not do God's will. (*Diary*, 666) What commandment did Lucifer disobey? What is heresy?
2) How is frequent personal inventory of our spiritual life helpful? (*Diary*, 672)
3) Sister wrote: "I am dying from the desire to save souls" (*Diary*, 679). Do we have this fervent desire?

LESSON GOALS:

At the end of the discussion, members should understand:

- The First Commandment, and how we disobey it,
- Personal inventory, not judgment of others, is necessary for spiritual advancement.

Week Eighty-three — *Diary*, 684-697

ADDITIONAL READING ASSIGNMENT TO PREPARE FOR THIS WEEK:

Scripture — Eph 4:22, 24; Tob 12:8-10
Catechism — #946-959, 1471-1479

WEEK OVERVIEW:

The promises of The Divine Mercy Chaplet, the Communion of Saints, and the role of suffering are discussed in the readings.

LEARNING AND DISCUSSION:

1) What are the promises of the Chaplet? (*Diary*, 687)
2) What is the Communion of Saints? (*Diary*, 689) What are indulgences?
3) How can interior sufferings be of value to our personal holiness? (*Diary*, 694)

LESSON GOALS:

At the end of the discussion, members should understand:

- Why we are to recite the Chaplet unceasingly,
- The Communion of Saints and the Church Triumphant,
- The doctrine and practice of indulgences.

Week Eighty-four — *Diary*, 698-715

ADDITIONAL READING ASSIGNMENT TO PREPARE FOR THIS WEEK:

Scripture — Lk 5:5-7; Heb 4:16; 2 Cor 5:7
Catechism — 1033, 391-392, 334-335

WEEK OVERVIEW:

The Feast of Mercy and associated promises, and the existence of Satan and hell are reviewed.

LEARNING AND DISCUSSION:

1) Why is the Feast of Mercy so important? (*Diary*, 690)
2) How is fear impossible if we trust? (*Diary*, 712)
3) How does Saint Faustina act when Satan entered her room? (*Diary*, 713) Does hell exist?

LESSON GOALS:

At the end of the discussion, members should understand:

- The Importance of the Feast of Mercy,
- The existence of Satan and hell.

Week Eighty-five — *Diary*, 716-736

ADDITIONAL READING ASSIGNMENT TO PREPARE FOR THIS WEEK:

Scripture — Mk 9:23; Jer 17:7; Tit 3:5; Psalm 119:165; Phil 4:7
Catechism — #227

WEEK OVERVIEW:

The benefit of trust in God is the theme of the week.

LEARNING AND DISCUSSION:

1) Discuss how trust opens floodgates of God's mercy and grace to one's soul (*Diary*, 718).
2) Discuss the line, **The greater the sinner, the greater the right he has to My mercy** (*Diary*, 723).
3) How do we find peace by submitting to God's holy will? (*Diary*, 724)

LESSON GOALS:

At the end of the discussion, members should understand:

- The value of trust in our lives,
- That all have a right to His mercy,
- That we can share God's mercy through works of mercy.

Week Eighty-six — *Diary*, 737-750

ADDITIONAL READING ASSIGNMENT TO
PREPARE FOR THIS WEEK:

Scripture — Jas 2:17, 24, 5:19
Catechism — #633, 1033, 1037

WEEK OVERVIEW:

The existence of hell, ways to exercise mercy, and promises associated with the Image are discussed this week.

LEARNING AND DISCUSSION:

1) Does God condemn the soul to hell? What were the seven tortures she saw? (*Diary*, 741)
2) What were the Lord's demands? What three ways can we exercise mercy? (*Diary*, 742)
3) What are the promises related to the Image? (*Diary*, 742)

LESSON GOALS:

At the end of the discussion, members should understand:

- Why we condemn ourselves to hell,
- That mercy is a demand, and not a request of the Lord,
- Ways of expressing mercy as a group and individually.

Week Eighty-seven — *Diary*, 751-764

ADDITIONAL READING ASSIGNMENT TO PREPARE FOR THIS WEEK:

Scripture — 2 Cor 6:10; 1 Pet 2:21,4:1; Jas 4:6
Catechism — 1866, 2540, 2094

WEEK OVERVIEW:

Suffering as gift, and personal pride as an obstacle to heroic virtue, are topics for the week.

LEARNING AND DISCUSSION:

1) How can suffering be a gift? (*Diary*, 756)
2) How does humility draw God to my soul? (*Diary*, 758)
3) Do we know our own virtues? Why must we strive for heroic virtues? (*Diary*, 758)
4) "Pay no attention to human opinion" (*Diary*, 763). Why do most of us struggle with that?

LESSON GOALS:

At the end of the discussion, members should understand:

- The role of pride in retarding our spiritual growth,
- Suffering as gift.

Week Eighty-eight — *Diary*, 765-777

ADDITIONAL READING ASSIGNMENT TO PREPARE FOR THIS WEEK:

Scripture — 2 Cor 11:23 to 12:1-10
Catechism — #2560-2561

WEEK OVERVIEW:

The beauty of heaven is the main theme for the week.

LEARNING AND DISCUSSION:

1) How are we to defend children from evil? (*Diary*, 765)
2) What is the thermometer that measures the love of God in a soul? (*Diary*, 774)
3) What awaits us in heaven? (*Diary*, 777)

LESSON GOALS:

At the end of the discussion, members should understand:

- The need to educate our youth properly in the Faith,
- The beauty of heaven and what awaits the faithful,
- The relationship of suffering and God's love.

Week Eighty-nine — *Diary*, 778-795

ADDITIONAL READING ASSIGNMENT TO PREPARE FOR THIS WEEK:

Scripture — 1 Pet 1:3-9, 4:1-2
Catechism — #1024, 1508

WEEK OVERVIEW:

The need for silence, humility, and suffering as combat are themes for this week.

LEARNING AND DISCUSSION:

1) Describe heaven as Saint Faustina experienced it.
2) How does Saint Faustina deal with sickness? Why does she describe it as combat? (*Diary*, 783)
3) In her Advent preparation, what two virtues does she pursue? How can we apply them?

LESSON GOALS:

At the end of the discussion, members should understand:

- The importance of humility and holy silence,
- Suffering or trial in this valley of tears,
- Splendor of heaven for those who are faithful.

Week Ninety — *Diary*, 796-815

ADDITIONAL READING ASSIGNMENT TO PREPARE FOR THIS WEEK:

Scripture — 1 Pet 5:7; Ps 24
Catechism — #2517-2518

WEEK OVERVIEW:

Topics for discussion include The Chaplet Novena to be said before the Feast of Mercy, the need for frequent Confession, and purity of intention.

LEARNING AND DISCUSSION:

1) Jesus told us to speak to Him about everything. To what does He compare the pleasure of hearing these things? (*Diary*, 797)
2) How do we proceed when things are uncertain? What is the important factor as God sees it? (*Diary*, 800)
3) Discuss the power of the Chaplet said for the dying. (*Diary*, 810)

LESSON GOALS:

At the end of the discussion, members should understand:

- The magnitude of the promises associated with the recitation of The Divine Mercy Chaplet,
- The Novena before the Feast of Mercy,
- The importance of purity of intention in our daily activities.

Week Ninety-one — *Diary*, 816-832

ADDITIONAL READING ASSIGNMENT TO PREPARE FOR THIS WEEK:

Scripture — Mt 3:1-3; Ps 32, Mt 5:24; 2 Mac 12:43
Catechism — #1435, 1446, 1456-1458

WEEK OVERVIEW:

The Sacrament of Reconciliation is the main theme in the readings for the week.

LEARNING AND DISCUSSION:

1) Do we realize our need for frequent confession, as a means of sanctification, providing a "clear path" to God? (*Diary*, 817)
2) Do we understand the importance of praying the Chaplet for the dying? (*Diary*, 820 and 828)
3) What about offering our sufferings in reparation for others? (*Diary*, 818)
4) What entry touched you this week?

LESSON GOALS:

At the end of the discussion, members should understand:

- The gift of the Sacrament of Reconciliation,
- The concept of offering sufferings up for salvation of souls.

Week Ninety-two — *Diary*, 833-843

ADDITIONAL READING ASSIGNMENT TO PREPARE FOR THIS WEEK:

Scripture — Mt 22:34-42; Eph 6:10-17; Ps 42; Ps 63
Catechism — #273, 274

WEEK OVERVIEW:

The necessity of reliance upon God, and how we can get to better know Him, are the topics for the week.

LEARNING AND DISCUSSION:

1) Do we rely on God for our source of strength and power, putting on His armor to wage war against sin? (*Diary*, 838).
2) How can we deepen our love and longing for the Lord? How can we get to know Him more intimately? (*Diary*, 841 & 843).

LESSON GOALS:

At the end of the discussion, members should understand:

- The need for reliance upon God,
- The importance of praying for the suffering,
- The need to know Our Lord in a more personal way.

Week Ninety-three — *Diary*, 844-855

ADDITIONAL READING ASSIGNMENT TO PREPARE FOR THIS WEEK:

Scripture — Lk 21:34-36; Mk 13:32; Mt 25:1; 2 Chr 30:9; Eph 2:4

Catechism — #674, 218-221

WEEK OVERVIEW:

The topics for the week include the importance of being in grace and ready to meet the Lord, and why we should take refuge in the Fount of God's Mercy.

LEARNING AND DISCUSSION:

1) Discuss how we should strive to be ready to meet Christ, as none of us is assured of tomorrow (*Diary*, 854).
2) Why do we find it difficult at times to realize how loving and merciful God truly is? (*Diary*, 848 & 853)
3) How are the sacraments a place of refuge, rich in God's mercy? (*Diary*, 848)

LESSON GOALS:

At the end of the discussion, members should understand:

- The need for a sacramental life in order to be ready for Our Lord,
- That God is love, and is always faithful to us.

Week Ninety-four — *Diary*, 856-868

ADDITIONAL READING ASSIGNMENT TO PREPARE FOR THIS WEEK:

Scripture — Mt 24:9; Lk 9:24; Eph 6:18
Catechism — #2473, 2725, 2744

WEEK OVERVIEW:

The types of martyrdom, prayer, and how Our Lord uses them to reside in our hearts are topics for the week.

LEARNING AND DISCUSSION:

1) What are the different types of martyrdom? (*Diary*, 856) What gave the saints the strength to endure this total sacrifice of self?
2) How can we cultivate a richer prayer life? (Time, commitment, etc.)
3) Do we realize God wishes to repose in our own souls? How should we prepare a place for Him? (*Diary*, 866)

LESSON GOALS:

At the end of the discussion, members should understand:

- The necessity of a healthy prayer life,
- The necessity of bearing witness of the Truth to those around us.

Week Ninety-five — *Diary*, 869-881

ADDITIONAL READING ASSIGNMENT TO PREPARE FOR THIS WEEK:

Scripture — Rom 1:9; Phil 1:3,4; Heb 7:25
Catechism — #2647, 1374, 1032

WEEK OVERVIEW:

Dying souls, purgatory, the need of intercessory prayer, and the Real Presence are themes for the week.

LEARNING AND DISCUSSION:

1) How do the prayers of intercession make us more Christ-like? (*Diary*, 870)
2) How can we as individuals, or as a group, help spread the truth of Christ's True Presence in the Eucharist?
3) Why are the souls of the dying especially in need of our aid and intercession?

LESSON GOALS:

At the end of the discussion, members should understand:

- The importance of prayer,
- The need to evangelize the beauty of our faith, especially the gift of the Eucharist.

Week Ninety-six — *Diary*, 882-897

ADDITIONAL READING ASSIGNMENT TO PREPARE FOR THIS WEEK:

Scripture — Col 3:1-2; 1 Pet 1:3-9
Catechism — #2613, 2629, 2634

WEEK OVERVIEW:

Doing the little things in life well, the necessity of silence, are topics this week.

LEARNING AND DISCUSSION:

1) How do we access the "world of the spirit"? (*Diary*, 884) — What is the role of faith?
2) Think of ways our "interior life" can give us strength in our vocation, as we try to do the little things well.
3) Discuss the wisdom of silence in Diary paragraph 888. What is contemplative prayer?

LESSON GOALS:

At the end of the discussion, members should understand:

- How union with God allows us to accomplish little things well,
- How our day should be continuous prayer.

Week Ninety-seven — *Diary*, 898-914

ADDITIONAL READING ASSIGNMENT TO PREPARE FOR THIS WEEK:

Scripture — Phil 3:12-14; 1 Cor 15:58; Jn 14:16,17,20
Catechism — #736, 2015

WEEK OVERVIEW:

The Holy Trinity, fruits of the Holy Spirit, and the virtue of patience are topics for the week.

LEARNING AND DISCUSSION:

1) Do we ask the Holy Spirit to bring every purpose God has for our lives to fulfillment? (*Diary*, 897)
2) Why does patience with oneself and others seem difficult to attain? (*Diary*, 900)
3) Discuss the mystery of the Trinity. (*Diary*, 911)

LESSON GOALS:

At the end of the discussion, members should understand:

- The Church teaching on the Trinity,
- The fruits of the Holy Spirit,
- The virtue of patience.

Week Ninety-eight — Read article on Our Call to Holiness

ADDITIONAL READING ASSIGNMENT TO PREPARE FOR THIS WEEK:

Scripture — Ps 37:28, Eph 2:19, 2 Thess 1:10
Catechism — #2013-2014, 2028-2029

WEEK OVERVIEW:

Our own call to holiness is the theme for the week. We are all "saints under construction."

LEARNING AND DISCUSSION:

1) Is holiness a goal only for religious?
2) What is the major obstacle to trust?
3) St. Faustina always gave thanks. Do we find ourselves always asking God for something instead of giving thanks?

LESSON GOALS:

At the end of the discussion, members should understand:

- Understand the personal call to holiness
- Understand the need to give thanks
- Understand that fear is a great obstacle to trust and spiritual progress

WEEK Ninety-nine — *Diary*, 915-929

ADDITIONAL READING ASSIGNMENT TO PREPARE FOR THIS WEEK

Scripture — Jas 5:12; Lk 2:34 -35; Mt 2:13-14, Lk 2:43-45; Jn 19:25-27
Catechism — #847, 2468

WEEK OVERVIEW:

The readings discuss Our Lady and her suffering, the graces granted through the Divine Mercy image, and obedience.

LEARNING & DISCUSSION:

1) Saint Faustina wrote, (*Diary*, 915) "May the sword of suffering never break me." What were the seven sorrows of Mary, and how is she our role model in times of suffering?
2) What is Church teaching on non-Christians entering heaven?
3) In *Diary* entry #919, St. Faustina wrote, "I said what I had to say." Scripture tells us to let our yes be yes and no be no. Frequently, we do not speak the truth for a variety of reasons. Discuss how we often hold back from speaking truth in the workplace and home, and the reasons why.

LESSON GOALS:

- Better understand Mary as our Mother and role model.
- Understand Church teaching on heaven.
- Importance of speaking truth, always in love, in daily situations.

WEEK One-Hundred – *Diary*, 930-941

ADDITIONAL READING ASSIGNMENT TO PREPARE FOR THE WEEK

Scripture — Gal 5:16-24
Catechism — #817, 953, 1550, 1554, 1593-94

WEEKLY OVERVIEW:

The effects of sin and Sister Faustina's contact with the dying, and the greatness of the dignity and responsibility of the priest are topics for review.

LEARNING & DISCUSSION:

1) How does charity and sin effect the communion of believers? (Gal 5:16-24, Catechism #817 and 953)
2) Why is prayerful recitation of The Divine Mercy Chaplet, said with an attitude of trust in God's mercy, so necessary? (*Diary*, 929)
3) Does the presence of Christ in the priest preserve him from human weakness? (*Diary*, 1550). What are the three degrees of the Sacrament of Holy Orders? (Catechism #1554, 1593-4)

LESSON GOALS:
- Better understand the effect of love and sin on the community of believers.
- Understand the importance of prayer, especially The Divine Mercy chaplet.
- Appreciate the gift of the Sacrament of Holy Orders, and how God works through all of us in spite of shortcomings.

Made in the USA
Middletown, DE
03 January 2016